CELEBRATING THE FAMILY NAME OF PÉREZ

Celebrating the Family Name of Pérez

Walter the Educator

Silent King Books
a WhichHead Entertainment Imprint

Copyright © 2024 by Walter the Educator

All rights reserved. No part of this book may be reproduced in any manner whatsoever without written permission except in the case of brief quotations embodied in critical articles and reviews.

First Printing, 2024

Disclaimer

This book is a literary work; the story is not about specific persons, locations, situations, and/or circumstances unless mentioned in a historical context. Any resemblance to real persons, locations, situations, and/or circumstances is coincidental. This book is for entertainment and informational purposes only. The author and publisher offer this information without warranties expressed or implied. No matter the grounds, neither the author nor the publisher will be accountable for any losses, injuries, or other damages caused by the reader's use of this book. The use of this book acknowledges an understanding and acceptance of this disclaimer.

Celebrating the Family Name of Pérez is a memory book that belongs to the Celebrating Family Name Book Series by Walter the Educator. Collect them all and more books at WaltertheEducator.com

USE THE EXTRA SPACE TO DOCUMENT YOUR FAMILY MEMORIES THROUGHOUT THE YEARS

PÉREZ

From ancient lands where olive trees sway,

Celebrating the Family Name of

Pérez

In valleys kissed by the Andalusian sun,

The name Pérez was born, carved from clay,

A legacy of honor that cannot be undone.

Through cobblestone streets where shadows dance,

And whispers of history echo the past,

Pérez emerges, not by chance,

But through tales of resilience that last.

In the heart of the village, where stories are spun,

Where elders recount the deeds of the brave,

The Pérez name, like a rising sun,

Illuminates paths others crave.

It's more than a word, a string of sounds,

It's a banner of pride that we raise,

In fields where golden grain abounds,

Or in cities where ambition stays.

Celebrating the Family Name of
Pérez

From the mountains of Asturias so high,

To the beaches where the sea meets the shore,

The Pérez name soars in the sky,

A song that is cherished evermore.

Generations have carried this name like a torch,

Through battles fought, through storms weathered,

On every door, it leaves a scorch,

A mark of a family, tightly tethered.

Pérez, a name like the sturdy oak,

Roots deep in the earth, branches wide,

It stands tall, though it never spoke,

Its strength is something we can't hide.

In the laughter of children, the wisdom of age,

In the warmth of a mother's embrace,

Pérez is the ink on every page,

Of the book of life that we all chase.

It's in the sweat of hard day's work,

In the songs sung at the break of day,

It's the quiet smile, the knowing smirk,

It's the words of encouragement we say.

Celebrating the Family Name of
Pérez

Pérez is the fire in the forge of time,

Where iron will and heart combine,

It's the chorus in a ballad's rhyme,

It's the courage in every line.

ABOUT THE CREATOR

Walter the Educator is one of the pseudonyms for Walter Anderson. Formally educated in Chemistry, Business, and Education, he is an educator, an author, a diverse entrepreneur, and he is the son of a disabled war veteran. "Walter the Educator" shares his time between educating and creating. He holds interests and owns several creative projects that entertain, enlighten, enhance, and educate, hoping to inspire and motivate you. Follow, find new works, and stay up to date with Walter the Educator™

at WaltertheEducator.com

Milton Keynes UK
Ingram Content Group UK Ltd.
UKHW022013230824
447344UK00012B/731